I'm practicing self-love and self-care.
I value my journal.

If found, return to:

_____

INSERT NAME

OTHER GUIDED JOURNALS & DIARIES
by
KINYATTA E. GRAY

I Miss You...

Daily Writing Prompts for Reflection, Remembrance, and Spirit Renewal

The Queen's Manifestation Journal

Daily Writing Prompt for Manifesting the Life You Want

Fashionista's Travel Diary

A Guided Travel Diary for Travel Planning & Reflections

Budget & Shop

A Monthly Personal Budget & Expense Tracker for Young Adults

I'm Doing Me

The Ultimate Breakup Diary for Venting, Reflection & Spirit Renewal

My Life My Love My Truth

LGBTQ journal

While I'm Still Here

A Guided Expression Journal of Life, Love and Legacy for Those Preparing to Transition

Sexy Baby Mama

Self-Love | Self-Reflections | Spirit Renewal

My Crazy Teenage Life

The Ultimate Expression Diary for Venting, Self-Reflections and Self-Love

The "Hallelujah" Notes

I Am A Man. I Have Feelings.

A Guided 90-Day Self-Reflections & Gratitude Journal for Men

Kinyatta E. Gray is a Best-Selling Author, Travel Influencer and the CEO of FlightsInStilettos, LLC. Kinyatta is also the Chief Beach Towel Designer for the FlightsInStilettos Glam Girl Beach Towels.

Websites:

https://www.flightsinstilettos.com/

https://www.kinyattagray.com/

https://www.honoringmissbee.com/

Greetings,

Thank you for taking that step to purchase this journal. I realize you had many options and chose this one.

This guided journal aims to help you take care of your well-being.

Often, we have many obligations to take care of others, whether it's a spouse, aging parents, children, or even a demanding career. As a result, we feel valued and needed when caring for others and often don't factor in that we need self-care and self-love.

Self-care is not selfish. You may feel guilty at times for looking inward at your needs and addressing them. But keep in mind, you can't pour from an empty cup, and isn't it ideal to offer the best of you and not what's left of you?

You are worthy and deserve the best of you!

Take your time and think about what steps you're taking now to preserve yourself and how you can commit to showing up as your best self every day.

Practicing self-love and self-care takes time; however, if you commit to doing one self-love/care activity each day, those small changes will make a significant impact on your life.

Xo,

Kinyatta

"Your greatest responsibility is to love yourself and to know you are enough."

~UNKNOWN

What is "Self-Love"?

SELF-LOVE is regard for one's own well-being and happiness – which is considered a desirable characteristic.

What is "Self-Care"?

SELF-CARE is the practice of taking action to preserve or improve one's own health.

Examples of Self-Love

- Being true to yourself
- Prioritizing yourself
- Trusting yourself
- Setting boundaries
- Showing yourself grace and kindness
- Self-forgiveness

Examples of Physical and Mental Self-Care Activities

- Eating balanced and nutritious meals
- Sipping hot tea
- Sitting in the sunlight
- Walking/Exercising
- Getting adequate rest
- Spa days
- Relaxing Baths
- Burning Candles/Sage
- Date nights (with a love interest or friends)
- Journaling
- Reading
- Meditating
- Connecting with people that energize you
- Creating a Vision Board
- Writing/Drawing
- Traveling

Gratitude

Gratitude makes us more optimistic, increases happiness, and reduces depression. In addition, gratitude is the state of being willing to show appreciation and to return kindness.

Check all that apply to you and challenge yourself to add ten more elements in your life for which you are grateful.

- ☐ I am thankful for my mind, body, and spirit
- ☐ I am thankful for how I generate income and financial independence
- ☐ I am grateful for the relationships I have with family members and friends
- ☐ I am grateful for a companion, spouse, or significant other to share my life with
- ☐ I am grateful for my creativity and extraordinary talents
- ☐ I am grateful for others who perform services (dry cleaners, Uber drivers, etc.) that add convenience to my life
- ☐ I am grateful for the lessons I learn daily
- ☐ I am thankful for the autonomy to make critical life decisions
- ☐ I am grateful for having a reason to smile every day
- ☐ I am grateful for those who trust and believe in me
- ☐ _____
- ☐ _____
- ☐ _____
- ☐ _____
- ☐ _____
- ☐ _____
- ☐ _____
- ☐ _____
- ☐ _____
- ☐ _____

My Self-Care Vision Board

Add words, images or quotes that represent the self-care activities you will commit to.

My Self-Care Vision Board

Add words, images or quotes that represent the self-care activities you will commit to.

My Self-Care Vision Board

Add words, images or quotes that represent the self-care activities you will commit to.

30 Days of Self-Care

Hold yourself accountable for your well-being by committing to 30-days of self-care activities

	Date	Self-care Activity	Appointment Needed (Yes or No)	After completing this activity, I felt
1				
2				
3				
4				
5				
6				
7				
8				
9				
10				
11				
12				
13				
14				
15				
16				
17				
18				
19				
20				
21				
22				
23				
24				
25				
26				
27				
28				
29				
30				

Daily Self-Reflections

I woke up today and felt:

I looked in the mirror and felt:

I nourished my body today by eating:

I dedicated: _____ minutes/hours to physical activity today.

I Feel:

- ☐ Excited
- ☐ Anxious
- ☐ Renewed
- ☐ Exhausted
- ☐ Angry
- ☐ Stressed
- ☐ Peaceful
- ☐ Happy
- ☐ Unhappy

This energized me at work:

I interacted with these people and felt cared for, motivated and inspired:

I am willing to release:

I showed gratitude by:

I loved this today and will commit to doing more of it:

I showed myself love/care and acceptance by:

I learned this about myself today:

DATE:

_____

Daily Self-Reflections

	I Feel:
I woke up today and felt:	☐ Excited
	☐ Anxious
I looked in the mirror and felt:	☐ Renewed
	☐ Exhausted
	☐ Angry
I nourished my body today by eating:	☐ Stressed
	☐ Peaceful
	☐ Happy
I dedicated: _____ minutes/hours to physical activity today.	☐ Unhappy

This energized me at work:

I interacted with these people and felt cared for, motivated and inspired:

I am willing to release:

I showed gratitude by:

I loved this today and will commit to doing more of it:

I showed myself love/care and acceptance by:

I learned this about myself today:

Daily Self-Reflections

	I Feel:
I woke up today and felt:	☐ Excited
	☐ Anxious
I looked in the mirror and felt:	☐ Renewed
	☐ Exhausted
	☐ Angry
I nourished my body today by eating:	☐ Stressed
	☐ Peaceful
	☐ Happy
I dedicated: _____ minutes/hours to physical activity today.	☐ Unhappy

This energized me at work:

I interacted with these people and felt cared for, motivated and inspired:

I am willing to release:

I showed gratitude by:

I loved this today and will commit to doing more of it:

I showed myself love/care and acceptance by:

I learned this about myself today:

Daily Self-Reflections

	I Feel:
I woke up today and felt:	☐ Excited
	☐ Anxious
I looked in the mirror and felt:	☐ Renewed
	☐ Exhausted
	☐ Angry
I nourished my body today by eating:	☐ Stressed
	☐ Peaceful
	☐ Happy
I dedicated: _____ minutes/hours to physical activity today.	☐ Unhappy

This energized me at work:

I interacted with these people and felt cared for, motivated and inspired:

I am willing to release:

I showed gratitude by:

I loved this today and will commit to doing more of it:

I showed myself love/care and acceptance by:

I learned this about myself today:

DATE:
_____

Daily Self-Reflections

I woke up today and felt:	**I Feel:**
I looked in the mirror and felt:	☐ Excited ☐ Anxious ☐ Renewed ☐ Exhausted
I nourished my body today by eating:	☐ Angry ☐ Stressed ☐ Peaceful ☐ Happy
I dedicated: ___ minutes/hours to physical activity today.	☐ Unhappy

This energized me at work:

I interacted with these people and felt cared for, motivated and inspired:

I am willing to release:

I showed gratitude by:

I loved this today and will commit to doing more of it:

I showed myself love/care and acceptance by:

I learned this about myself today:

DATE:

_____

Daily Self-Reflections

I woke up today and felt:

I looked in the mirror and felt:

I nourished my body today by eating:

I dedicated: _____ minutes/hours to physical activity today.

I Feel:

☐ Excited
☐ Anxious
☐ Renewed
☐ Exhausted
☐ Angry
☐ Stressed
☐ Peaceful
☐ Happy
☐ Unhappy

This energized me at work:

I interacted with these people and felt cared for, motivated and inspired:

I am willing to release:

I showed gratitude by:

I loved this today and will commit to doing more of it:

I showed myself love/care and acceptance by:

I learned this about myself today:

Daily Self-Reflections

	I Feel:
I woke up today and felt:	☐ Excited
	☐ Anxious
I looked in the mirror and felt:	☐ Renewed
	☐ Exhausted
	☐ Angry
I nourished my body today by eating:	☐ Stressed
	☐ Peaceful
	☐ Happy
I dedicated: _____ minutes/hours to physical activity today.	☐ Unhappy

This energized me at work:

I interacted with these people and felt cared for, motivated and inspired:

I am willing to release:

I showed gratitude by:

I loved this today and will commit to doing more of it:

I showed myself love/care and acceptance by:

I learned this about myself today:

DATE:

_____

Daily Self-Reflections

I woke up today and felt:	**I Feel:**
	☐ Excited
	☐ Anxious
I looked in the mirror and felt:	☐ Renewed
	☐ Exhausted
	☐ Angry
I nourished my body today by eating:	☐ Stressed
	☐ Peaceful
	☐ Happy
I dedicated: _____ minutes/hours to physical activity today.	☐ Unhappy

This energized me at work:

I interacted with these people and felt cared for, motivated and inspired:

I am willing to release:

I showed gratitude by:

I loved this today and will commit to doing more of it:

I showed myself love/care and acceptance by:

I learned this about myself today:

Daily Self-Reflections

	I Feel:
I woke up today and felt:	☐ Excited
	☐ Anxious
I looked in the mirror and felt:	☐ Renewed
	☐ Exhausted
	☐ Angry
I nourished my body today by eating:	☐ Stressed
	☐ Peaceful
	☐ Happy
I dedicated: _____ minutes/hours to physical activity today.	☐ Unhappy

This energized me at work:

I interacted with these people and felt cared for, motivated and inspired:

I am willing to release:

I showed gratitude by:

I loved this today and will commit to doing more of it:

I showed myself love/care and acceptance by:

I learned this about myself today:

DATE:

_____

Daily Self-Reflections

I woke up today and felt:	**I Feel:**
	☐ Excited
	☐ Anxious
I looked in the mirror and felt:	☐ Renewed
	☐ Exhausted
	☐ Angry
I nourished my body today by eating:	☐ Stressed
	☐ Peaceful
	☐ Happy
I dedicated: _____ minutes/hours to physical activity today.	☐ Unhappy

This energized me at work:

I interacted with these people and felt cared for, motivated and inspired:

I am willing to release:

I showed gratitude by:

I loved this today and will commit to doing more of it:

I showed myself love/care and acceptance by:

I learned this about myself today:

Daily Self-Reflections

I woke up today and felt:	**I Feel:**
	☐ Excited
	☐ Anxious
I looked in the mirror and felt:	☐ Renewed
	☐ Exhausted
	☐ Angry
I nourished my body today by eating:	☐ Stressed
	☐ Peaceful
	☐ Happy
I dedicated: _____ minutes/hours to physical activity today.	☐ Unhappy

This energized me at work:

I interacted with these people and felt cared for, motivated and inspired:

I am willing to release:

I showed gratitude by:

I loved this today and will commit to doing more of it:

I showed myself love/care and acceptance by:

I learned this about myself today:

DATE:

_____

Daily Self-Reflections

I woke up today and felt:	**I Feel:**
	☐ Excited
	☐ Anxious
I looked in the mirror and felt:	☐ Renewed
	☐ Exhausted
	☐ Angry
I nourished my body today by eating:	☐ Stressed
	☐ Peaceful
	☐ Happy
I dedicated: _____ minutes/hours to physical activity today.	☐ Unhappy

This energized me at work:

I interacted with these people and felt cared for, motivated and inspired:

I am willing to release:

I showed gratitude by:

I loved this today and will commit to doing more of it:

I showed myself love/care and acceptance by:

I learned this about myself today:

Daily Self-Reflections

I woke up today and felt:	**I Feel:**
	☐ Excited
	☐ Anxious
I looked in the mirror and felt:	☐ Renewed
	☐ Exhausted
	☐ Angry
I nourished my body today by eating:	☐ Stressed
	☐ Peaceful
	☐ Happy
I dedicated: _____ minutes/hours to physical activity today.	☐ Unhappy

This energized me at work:

I interacted with these people and felt cared for, motivated and inspired:

I am willing to release:

I showed gratitude by:

I loved this today and will commit to doing more of it:

I showed myself love/care and acceptance by:

I learned this about myself today:

DATE:

_____

Daily Self-Reflections

I woke up today and felt:	**I Feel:**
	☐ Excited
	☐ Anxious
I looked in the mirror and felt:	☐ Renewed
	☐ Exhausted
	☐ Angry
I nourished my body today by eating:	☐ Stressed
	☐ Peaceful
	☐ Happy
I dedicated: _____ minutes/hours to physical activity today.	☐ Unhappy

This energized me at work:

I interacted with these people and felt cared for, motivated and inspired:

I am willing to release:

I showed gratitude by:

I loved this today and will commit to doing more of it:

I showed myself love/care and acceptance by:

I learned this about myself today:

Daily Self-Reflections

	I Feel:
I woke up today and felt:	☐ Excited
	☐ Anxious
I looked in the mirror and felt:	☐ Renewed
	☐ Exhausted
	☐ Angry
I nourished my body today by eating:	☐ Stressed
	☐ Peaceful
	☐ Happy
I dedicated: _____ minutes/hours to physical activity today.	☐ Unhappy

This energized me at work:

I interacted with these people and felt cared for, motivated and inspired:

I am willing to release:

I showed gratitude by:

I loved this today and will commit to doing more of it:

I showed myself love/care and acceptance by:

I learned this about myself today:

DATE:

_____

Daily Self-Reflections

I woke up today and felt:	**I Feel:**
	☐ Excited
	☐ Anxious
I looked in the mirror and felt:	☐ Renewed
	☐ Exhausted
	☐ Angry
I nourished my body today by eating:	☐ Stressed
	☐ Peaceful
	☐ Happy
I dedicated: _____ minutes/hours to physical activity today.	☐ Unhappy

This energized me at work:

I interacted with these people and felt cared for, motivated and inspired:

I am willing to release:

I showed gratitude by:

I loved this today and will commit to doing more of it:

I showed myself love/care and acceptance by:

I learned this about myself today:

Daily Self—Reflections

I woke up today and felt:

I looked in the mirror and felt:

I nourished my body today by eating:

I dedicated: _____ minutes/hours to physical activity today.

I Feel:

☐ Excited
☐ Anxious
☐ Renewed
☐ Exhausted
☐ Angry
☐ Stressed
☐ Peaceful
☐ Happy
☐ Unhappy

This energized me at work:

I interacted with these people and felt cared for, motivated and inspired:

I am willing to release:

I showed gratitude by:

I loved this today and will commit to doing more of it:

I showed myself love/care and acceptance by:

I learned this about myself today:

Daily Self-Reflections

I woke up today and felt:

I looked in the mirror and felt:

I nourished my body today by eating:

I dedicated: _____ minutes/hours to physical activity today.

I Feel:

☐ Excited
☐ Anxious
☐ Renewed
☐ Exhausted
☐ Angry
☐ Stressed
☐ Peaceful
☐ Happy
☐ Unhappy

This energized me at work:

I interacted with these people and felt cared for, motivated and inspired:

I am willing to release:

I showed gratitude by:

I loved this today and will commit to doing more of it:

I showed myself love/care and acceptance by:

I learned this about myself today:

Daily Self—Reflections

	I Feel:
I woke up today and felt:	☐ Excited
	☐ Anxious
I looked in the mirror and felt:	☐ Renewed
	☐ Exhausted
	☐ Angry
I nourished my body today by eating:	☐ Stressed
	☐ Peaceful
	☐ Happy
I dedicated: _____ minutes/hours to physical activity today.	☐ Unhappy

This energized me at work:

I interacted with these people and felt cared for, motivated and inspired:

I am willing to release:

I showed gratitude by:

I loved this today and will commit to doing more of it:

I showed myself love/care and acceptance by:

I learned this about myself today:

DATE:

_____

Daily Self-Reflections

I woke up today and felt:	**I Feel:**
	☐ Excited
	☐ Anxious
I looked in the mirror and felt:	☐ Renewed
	☐ Exhausted
	☐ Angry
I nourished my body today by eating:	☐ Stressed
	☐ Peaceful
	☐ Happy
I dedicated: ___ minutes/hours to physical activity today.	☐ Unhappy

This energized me at work:

I interacted with these people and felt cared for, motivated and inspired:

I am willing to release:

I showed gratitude by:

I loved this today and will commit to doing more of it:

I showed myself love/care and acceptance by:

I learned this about myself today:

Daily Self-Reflections

I woke up today and felt:

I looked in the mirror and felt:

I nourished my body today by eating:

I dedicated: _____ minutes/hours to physical activity today.

I Feel:

- ☐ Excited
- ☐ Anxious
- ☐ Renewed
- ☐ Exhausted
- ☐ Angry
- ☐ Stressed
- ☐ Peaceful
- ☐ Happy
- ☐ Unhappy

This energized me at work:

I interacted with these people and felt cared for, motivated and inspired:

I am willing to release:

I showed gratitude by:

I loved this today and will commit to doing more of it:

I showed myself love/care and acceptance by:

I learned this about myself today:

DATE:

_____

Daily Self-Reflections

	I Feel:
I woke up today and felt:	☐ Excited
	☐ Anxious
I looked in the mirror and felt:	☐ Renewed
	☐ Exhausted
	☐ Angry
I nourished my body today by eating:	☐ Stressed
	☐ Peaceful
	☐ Happy
I dedicated: _____ minutes/hours to physical activity today.	☐ Unhappy

This energized me at work:

I interacted with these people and felt cared for, motivated and inspired:

I am willing to release:

I showed gratitude by:

I loved this today and will commit to doing more of it:

I showed myself love/care and acceptance by:

I learned this about myself today:

DATE:
_____

Daily Self-Reflections

I woke up today and felt:	**I Feel:**
	☐ Excited
I looked in the mirror and felt:	☐ Anxious
	☐ Renewed
	☐ Exhausted
I nourished my body today by eating:	☐ Angry
	☐ Stressed
	☐ Peaceful
I dedicated: minutes/hours to physical activity today.	☐ Happy ☐ Unhappy

This energized me at work:

I interacted with these people and felt cared for, motivated and inspired:

I am willing to release:

I showed gratitude by:

I loved this today and will commit to doing more of it:

I showed myself love/care and acceptance by:

I learned this about myself today:

DATE:

_____

Daily Self—Reflections

	I Feel:
I woke up today and felt:	☐ Excited
	☐ Anxious
I looked in the mirror and felt:	☐ Renewed
	☐ Exhausted
	☐ Angry
I nourished my body today by eating:	☐ Stressed
	☐ Peaceful
	☐ Happy
I dedicated: _____ minutes/hours to physical activity today.	☐ Unhappy

This energized me at work:

I interacted with these people and felt cared for, motivated and inspired:

I am willing to release:

I showed gratitude by:

I loved this today and will commit to doing more of it:

I showed myself love/care and acceptance by:

I learned this about myself today:

Daily Self–Reflections

	I Feel:
I woke up today and felt:	☐ Excited
	☐ Anxious
I looked in the mirror and felt:	☐ Renewed
	☐ Exhausted
	☐ Angry
I nourished my body today by eating:	☐ Stressed
	☐ Peaceful
	☐ Happy
I dedicated: _____ minutes/hours to physical activity today.	☐ Unhappy

This energized me at work:

I interacted with these people and felt cared for, motivated and inspired:

I am willing to release:

I showed gratitude by:

I loved this today and will commit to doing more of it:

I showed myself love/care and acceptance by:

I learned this about myself today:

DATE:

_____

Daily Self-Reflections

I woke up today and felt:	**I Feel:**
	☐ Excited
	☐ Anxious
I looked in the mirror and felt:	☐ Renewed
	☐ Exhausted
	☐ Angry
I nourished my body today by eating:	☐ Stressed
	☐ Peaceful
	☐ Happy
I dedicated: _____ minutes/hours to physical activity today.	☐ Unhappy

This energized me at work:

I interacted with these people and felt cared for, motivated and inspired:

I am willing to release:

I showed gratitude by:

I loved this today and will commit to doing more of it:

I showed myself love/care and acceptance by:

I learned this about myself today:

DATE: _____

Daily Self-Reflections

	I Feel:
I woke up today and felt:	☐ Excited
	☐ Anxious
I looked in the mirror and felt:	☐ Renewed
	☐ Exhausted
	☐ Angry
I nourished my body today by eating:	☐ Stressed
	☐ Peaceful
	☐ Happy
I dedicated: _____ minutes/hours to physical activity today.	☐ Unhappy

This energized me at work:

I interacted with these people and felt cared for, motivated and inspired:

I am willing to release:

I showed gratitude by:

I loved this today and will commit to doing more of it:

I showed myself love/care and acceptance by:

I learned this about myself today:

DATE:

_____

Daily Self-Reflections

I woke up today and felt:	**I Feel:**
	☐ Excited
	☐ Anxious
I looked in the mirror and felt:	☐ Renewed
	☐ Exhausted
	☐ Angry
I nourished my body today by eating:	☐ Stressed
	☐ Peaceful
	☐ Happy
I dedicated: minutes/hours to physical activity today.	☐ Unhappy

This energized me at work:

I interacted with these people and felt cared for, motivated and inspired:

I am willing to release:

I showed gratitude by:

I loved this today and will commit to doing more of it:

I showed myself love/care and acceptance by:

I learned this about myself today:

DATE: _____

Daily Self-Reflections

I woke up today and felt:

I looked in the mirror and felt:

I nourished my body today by eating:

I dedicated: _____ minutes/hours to physical activity today.

I Feel:
- ☐ Excited
- ☐ Anxious
- ☐ Renewed
- ☐ Exhausted
- ☐ Angry
- ☐ Stressed
- ☐ Peaceful
- ☐ Happy
- ☐ Unhappy

This energized me at work:

I interacted with these people and felt cared for, motivated and inspired:

I am willing to release:

I showed gratitude by:

I loved this today and will commit to doing more of it:

I showed myself love/care and acceptance by:

I learned this about myself today:

DATE:
_____

Daily Self-Reflections

I woke up today and felt:

I looked in the mirror and felt:

I nourished my body today by eating:

I dedicated: _____ minutes/hours to physical activity today.

I Feel:

☐ Excited
☐ Anxious
☐ Renewed
☐ Exhausted
☐ Angry
☐ Stressed
☐ Peaceful
☐ Happy
☐ Unhappy

This energized me at work:

I interacted with these people and felt cared for, motivated and inspired:

I am willing to release:

I showed gratitude by:

I loved this today and will commit to doing more of it:

I showed myself love/care and acceptance by:

I learned this about myself today:

Daily Self-Reflections

I woke up today and felt:	**I Feel:**
	☐ Excited
	☐ Anxious
I looked in the mirror and felt:	☐ Renewed
	☐ Exhausted
	☐ Angry
I nourished my body today by eating:	☐ Stressed
	☐ Peaceful
	☐ Happy
I dedicated: _____ minutes/hours to physical activity today.	☐ Unhappy

This energized me at work:

I interacted with these people and felt cared for, motivated and inspired:

I am willing to release:

I showed gratitude by:

I loved this today and will commit to doing more of it:

I showed myself love/care and acceptance by:

I learned this about myself today:

Daily Self-Reflections

I woke up today and felt:

I Feel:

☐ Excited

☐ Anxious

I looked in the mirror and felt:

☐ Renewed

☐ Exhausted

☐ Angry

I nourished my body today by eating:

☐ Stressed

☐ Peaceful

☐ Happy

I dedicated: _____ minutes/hours to physical activity today.

☐ Unhappy

This energized me at work:

I interacted with these people and felt cared for, motivated and inspired:

I am willing to release:

I showed gratitude by:

I loved this today and will commit to doing more of it:

I showed myself love/care and acceptance by:

I learned this about myself today:

DATE:

_____

Daily Self-Reflections

	I Feel:
I woke up today and felt:	☐ Excited
	☐ Anxious
I looked in the mirror and felt:	☐ Renewed
	☐ Exhausted
	☐ Angry
I nourished my body today by eating:	☐ Stressed
	☐ Peaceful
	☐ Happy
I dedicated: minutes/hours to physical activity today.	☐ Unhappy

This energized me at work:

I interacted with these people and felt cared for, motivated and inspired:

I am willing to release:

I showed gratitude by:

I loved this today and will commit to doing more of it:

I showed myself love/care and acceptance by:

I learned this about myself today:

DATE:

_____

Daily Self-Reflections

I woke up today and felt:	**I Feel:**
	☐ Excited
	☐ Anxious
I looked in the mirror and felt:	☐ Renewed
	☐ Exhausted
	☐ Angry
I nourished my body today by eating:	☐ Stressed
	☐ Peaceful
	☐ Happy
I dedicated: _____ minutes/hours to physical activity today.	☐ Unhappy

This energized me at work:

I interacted with these people and felt cared for, motivated and inspired:

I am willing to release:

I showed gratitude by:

I loved this today and will commit to doing more of it:

I showed myself love/care and acceptance by:

I learned this about myself today:

DATE:
_____

Daily Self-Reflections

I woke up today and felt:	**I Feel:**
	☐ Excited
	☐ Anxious
I looked in the mirror and felt:	☐ Renewed
	☐ Exhausted
	☐ Angry
I nourished my body today by eating:	☐ Stressed
	☐ Peaceful
	☐ Happy
I dedicated: _____ minutes/hours to physical activity today.	☐ Unhappy

This energized me at work:

I interacted with these people and felt cared for, motivated and inspired:

I am willing to release:

I showed gratitude by:

I loved this today and will commit to doing more of it:

I showed myself love/care and acceptance by:

I learned this about myself today:

Daily Self-Reflections

	I Feel:
I woke up today and felt:	☐ Excited
	☐ Anxious
I looked in the mirror and felt:	☐ Renewed
	☐ Exhausted
	☐ Angry
I nourished my body today by eating:	☐ Stressed
	☐ Peaceful
	☐ Happy
I dedicated: _____ minutes/hours to physical activity today.	☐ Unhappy

This energized me at work:

I interacted with these people and felt cared for, motivated and inspired:

I am willing to release:

I showed gratitude by:

I loved this today and will commit to doing more of it:

I showed myself love/care and acceptance by:

I learned this about myself today:

Daily Self-Reflections

	I Feel:
I woke up today and felt:	☐ Excited
	☐ Anxious
I looked in the mirror and felt:	☐ Renewed
	☐ Exhausted
	☐ Angry
I nourished my body today by eating:	☐ Stressed
	☐ Peaceful
	☐ Happy
I dedicated: _____ minutes/hours to physical activity today.	☐ Unhappy

This energized me at work:

I interacted with these people and felt cared for, motivated and inspired:

I am willing to release:

I showed gratitude by:

I loved this today and will commit to doing more of it:

I showed myself love/care and acceptance by:

I learned this about myself today:

DATE:

_____

Daily Self-Reflections

I woke up today and felt:

I Feel:

I looked in the mirror and felt:

- ☐ Excited
- ☐ Anxious
- ☐ Renewed
- ☐ Exhausted
- ☐ Angry

I nourished my body today by eating:

- ☐ Stressed
- ☐ Peaceful
- ☐ Happy

I dedicated: _____ minutes/hours to physical activity today.

- ☐ Unhappy

This energized me at work:

I interacted with these people and felt cared for, motivated and inspired:

I am willing to release:

I showed gratitude by:

I loved this today and will commit to doing more of it:

I showed myself love/care and acceptance by:

I learned this about myself today:

DATE:

_____

Daily Self-Reflections

I woke up today and felt:	**I Feel:**
	☐ Excited
	☐ Anxious
I looked in the mirror and felt:	☐ Renewed
	☐ Exhausted
	☐ Angry
I nourished my body today by eating:	☐ Stressed
	☐ Peaceful
	☐ Happy
I dedicated: minutes/hours to physical activity today.	☐ Unhappy

This energized me at work:

I interacted with these people and felt cared for, motivated and inspired:

I am willing to release:

I showed gratitude by:

I loved this today and will commit to doing more of it:

I showed myself love/care and acceptance by:

I learned this about myself today:

DATE:
_____

Daily Self-Reflections

I woke up today and felt:	**I Feel:**
	☐ Excited
	☐ Anxious
I looked in the mirror and felt:	☐ Renewed
	☐ Exhausted
	☐ Angry
I nourished my body today by eating:	☐ Stressed
	☐ Peaceful
	☐ Happy
I dedicated: _____ minutes/hours to physical activity today.	☐ Unhappy

This energized me at work:

I interacted with these people and felt cared for, motivated and inspired:

I am willing to release:

I showed gratitude by:

I loved this today and will commit to doing more of it:

I showed myself love/care and acceptance by:

I learned this about myself today:

Daily Self-Reflections

	I Feel:
I woke up today and felt:	☐ Excited
	☐ Anxious
I looked in the mirror and felt:	☐ Renewed
	☐ Exhausted
	☐ Angry
I nourished my body today by eating:	☐ Stressed
	☐ Peaceful
	☐ Happy
I dedicated: _____ minutes/hours to physical activity today.	☐ Unhappy

This energized me at work:

I interacted with these people and felt cared for, motivated and inspired:

I am willing to release:

I showed gratitude by:

I loved this today and will commit to doing more of it:

I showed myself love/care and acceptance by:

I learned this about myself today:

Daily Self-Reflections

	I Feel:
I woke up today and felt:	☐ Excited
	☐ Anxious
I looked in the mirror and felt:	☐ Renewed
	☐ Exhausted
	☐ Angry
I nourished my body today by eating:	☐ Stressed
	☐ Peaceful
	☐ Happy
I dedicated: _____ minutes/hours to physical activity today.	☐ Unhappy

This energized me at work:

I interacted with these people and felt cared for, motivated and inspired:

I am willing to release:

I showed gratitude by:

I loved this today and will commit to doing more of it:

I showed myself love/care and acceptance by:

I learned this about myself today:

DATE:
_____

Daily Self—Reflections

	I Feel:
I woke up today and felt:	☐ Excited
	☐ Anxious
I looked in the mirror and felt:	☐ Renewed
	☐ Exhausted
	☐ Angry
I nourished my body today by eating:	☐ Stressed
	☐ Peaceful
	☐ Happy
I dedicated: _____ minutes/hours to physical activity today.	☐ Unhappy

This energized me at work:

I interacted with these people and felt cared for, motivated and inspired:

I am willing to release:

I showed gratitude by:

I loved this today and will commit to doing more of it:

I showed myself love/care and acceptance by:

I learned this about myself today:

DATE:

_____

Daily Self-Reflections

I woke up today and felt:	**I Feel:**
	☐ Excited
	☐ Anxious
I looked in the mirror and felt:	☐ Renewed
	☐ Exhausted
	☐ Angry
I nourished my body today by eating:	☐ Stressed
	☐ Peaceful
	☐ Happy
I dedicated: _____ minutes/hours to physical activity today.	☐ Unhappy

This energized me at work:

I interacted with these people and felt cared for, motivated and inspired:

I am willing to release:

I showed gratitude by:

I loved this today and will commit to doing more of it:

I showed myself love/care and acceptance by:

I learned this about myself today:

Daily Self–Reflections

	I Feel:
I woke up today and felt:	☐ Excited
	☐ Anxious
I looked in the mirror and felt:	☐ Renewed
	☐ Exhausted
	☐ Angry
I nourished my body today by eating:	☐ Stressed
	☐ Peaceful
	☐ Happy
I dedicated: _____ minutes/hours to physical activity today.	☐ Unhappy

This energized me at work:

I interacted with these people and felt cared for, motivated and inspired:

I am willing to release:

I showed gratitude by:

I loved this today and will commit to doing more of it:

I showed myself love/care and acceptance by:

I learned this about myself today:

DATE: _____

Daily Self-Reflections

I woke up today and felt:	**I Feel:**
	☐ Excited
	☐ Anxious
I looked in the mirror and felt:	☐ Renewed
	☐ Exhausted
	☐ Angry
I nourished my body today by eating:	☐ Stressed
	☐ Peaceful
	☐ Happy
I dedicated: minutes/hours to physical activity today.	☐ Unhappy

This energized me at work:

I interacted with these people and felt cared for, motivated and inspired:

I am willing to release:

I showed gratitude by:

I loved this today and will commit to doing more of it:

I showed myself love/care and acceptance by:

I learned this about myself today:

Daily Self-Reflections

I woke up today and felt:

I looked in the mirror and felt:

I nourished my body today by eating:

I dedicated: _____ minutes/hours to physical activity today.

I Feel:
- ☐ Excited
- ☐ Anxious
- ☐ Renewed
- ☐ Exhausted
- ☐ Angry
- ☐ Stressed
- ☐ Peaceful
- ☐ Happy
- ☐ Unhappy

This energized me at work:

I interacted with these people and felt cared for, motivated and inspired:

I am willing to release:

I showed gratitude by:

I loved this today and will commit to doing more of it:

I showed myself love/care and acceptance by:

I learned this about myself today:

DATE:
_____

Daily Self-Reflections

I woke up today and felt:	**I Feel:**
	☐ Excited
	☐ Anxious
I looked in the mirror and felt:	☐ Renewed
	☐ Exhausted
	☐ Angry
I nourished my body today by eating:	☐ Stressed
	☐ Peaceful
	☐ Happy
I dedicated: _____ minutes/hours to physical activity today.	☐ Unhappy

This energized me at work:

I interacted with these people and felt cared for, motivated and inspired:

I am willing to release:

I showed gratitude by:

I loved this today and will commit to doing more of it:

I showed myself love/care and acceptance by:

I learned this about myself today:

DATE:

_____

Daily Self-Reflections

I woke up today and felt:	**I Feel:**
	☐ Excited
	☐ Anxious
I looked in the mirror and felt:	☐ Renewed
	☐ Exhausted
	☐ Angry
I nourished my body today by eating:	☐ Stressed
	☐ Peaceful
	☐ Happy
I dedicated: _____ minutes/hours to physical activity today.	☐ Unhappy

This energized me at work:

I interacted with these people and felt cared for, motivated and inspired:

I am willing to release:

I showed gratitude by:

I loved this today and will commit to doing more of it:

I showed myself love/care and acceptance by:

I learned this about myself today:

DATE:

_____

Daily Self-Reflections

I woke up today and felt:	**I Feel:**
	☐ Excited
	☐ Anxious
I looked in the mirror and felt:	☐ Renewed
	☐ Exhausted
	☐ Angry
I nourished my body today by eating:	☐ Stressed
	☐ Peaceful
	☐ Happy
I dedicated: minutes/hours to physical activity today.	☐ Unhappy

This energized me at work:

I interacted with these people and felt cared for, motivated and inspired:

I am willing to release:

I showed gratitude by:

I loved this today and will commit to doing more of it:

I showed myself love/care and acceptance by:

I learned this about myself today:

Daily Self-Reflections

I woke up today and felt:

I looked in the mirror and felt:

I nourished my body today by eating:

I dedicated: _____ minutes/hours to physical activity today.

I Feel:

☐ Excited
☐ Anxious
☐ Renewed
☐ Exhausted
☐ Angry
☐ Stressed
☐ Peaceful
☐ Happy
☐ Unhappy

This energized me at work:

I interacted with these people and felt cared for, motivated and inspired:

I am willing to release:

I showed gratitude by:

I loved this today and will commit to doing more of it:

I showed myself love/care and acceptance by:

I learned this about myself today:

DATE:

_____

Daily Self-Reflections

I woke up today and felt:	**I Feel:** ☐ Excited ☐ Anxious
I looked in the mirror and felt:	☐ Renewed ☐ Exhausted ☐ Angry
I nourished my body today by eating:	☐ Stressed ☐ Peaceful ☐ Happy
I dedicated: _____ minutes/hours to physical activity today.	☐ Unhappy

This energized me at work:

I interacted with these people and felt cared for, motivated and inspired:

I am willing to release:

I showed gratitude by:

I loved this today and will commit to doing more of it:

I showed myself love/care and acceptance by:

I learned this about myself today:

Daily Self-Reflections

	I Feel:
I woke up today and felt:	☐ Excited
	☐ Anxious
I looked in the mirror and felt:	☐ Renewed
	☐ Exhausted
	☐ Angry
I nourished my body today by eating:	☐ Stressed
	☐ Peaceful
	☐ Happy
I dedicated: ____ minutes/hours to physical activity today.	☐ Unhappy

This energized me at work:

I interacted with these people and felt cared for, motivated and inspired:

I am willing to release:

I showed gratitude by:

I loved this today and will commit to doing more of it:

I showed myself love/care and acceptance by:

I learned this about myself today:

DATE:

_____

Daily Self-Reflections

I woke up today and felt:	**I Feel:** ☐ Excited ☐ Anxious
I looked in the mirror and felt:	☐ Renewed ☐ Exhausted ☐ Angry
I nourished my body today by eating:	☐ Stressed ☐ Peaceful ☐ Happy
I dedicated: _____ minutes/hours to physical activity today.	☐ Unhappy

This energized me at work:

I interacted with these people and felt cared for, motivated and inspired:

I am willing to release:

I showed gratitude by:

I loved this today and will commit to doing more of it:

I showed myself love/care and acceptance by:

I learned this about myself today:

DATE:
_____

Daily Self-Reflections

	I Feel:
I woke up today and felt:	☐ Excited
	☐ Anxious
I looked in the mirror and felt:	☐ Renewed
	☐ Exhausted
	☐ Angry
I nourished my body today by eating:	☐ Stressed
	☐ Peaceful
	☐ Happy
I dedicated: _____ minutes/hours to physical activity today.	☐ Unhappy

This energized me at work:

I interacted with these people and felt cared for, motivated and inspired:

I am willing to release:

I showed gratitude by:

I loved this today and will commit to doing more of it:

I showed myself love/care and acceptance by:

I learned this about myself today:

DATE:

_____

Daily Self-Reflections

I woke up today and felt:	**I Feel:**
	☐ Excited
	☐ Anxious
I looked in the mirror and felt:	☐ Renewed
	☐ Exhausted
	☐ Angry
I nourished my body today by eating:	☐ Stressed
	☐ Peaceful
	☐ Happy
I dedicated:_____ minutes/hours to physical activity today.	☐ Unhappy

This energized me at work:

I interacted with these people and felt cared for, motivated and inspired:

I am willing to release:

I showed gratitude by:

I loved this today and will commit to doing more of it:

I showed myself love/care and acceptance by:

I learned this about myself today:

Daily Self-Reflections

I woke up today and felt:

I looked in the mirror and felt:

I nourished my body today by eating:

I dedicated: _____ minutes/hours to physical activity today.

I Feel:
- ☐ Excited
- ☐ Anxious
- ☐ Renewed
- ☐ Exhausted
- ☐ Angry
- ☐ Stressed
- ☐ Peaceful
- ☐ Happy
- ☐ Unhappy

This energized me at work:

I interacted with these people and felt cared for, motivated and inspired:

I am willing to release:

I showed gratitude by:

I loved this today and will commit to doing more of it:

I showed myself love/care and acceptance by:

I learned this about myself today:

Daily Self-Reflections

	I Feel:
I woke up today and felt:	☐ Excited
	☐ Anxious
I looked in the mirror and felt:	☐ Renewed
	☐ Exhausted
	☐ Angry
I nourished my body today by eating:	☐ Stressed
	☐ Peaceful
	☐ Happy
I dedicated: _____ minutes/hours to physical activity today.	☐ Unhappy

This energized me at work:

I interacted with these people and felt cared for, motivated and inspired:

I am willing to release:

I showed gratitude by:

I loved this today and will commit to doing more of it:

I showed myself love/care and acceptance by:

I learned this about myself today:

DATE: _____ # Daily Self-Reflections

I woke up today and felt:	**I Feel:**
	☐ Excited
I looked in the mirror and felt:	☐ Anxious
	☐ Renewed
	☐ Exhausted
I nourished my body today by eating:	☐ Angry
	☐ Stressed
	☐ Peaceful
	☐ Happy
I dedicated: _____ minutes/hours to physical activity today.	☐ Unhappy

This energized me at work:

I interacted with these people and felt cared for, motivated and inspired:

I am willing to release:

I showed gratitude by:

I loved this today and will commit to doing more of it:

I showed myself love/care and acceptance by:

I learned this about myself today:

Daily Self—Reflections

	I Feel:
I woke up today and felt:	☐ Excited
	☐ Anxious
I looked in the mirror and felt:	☐ Renewed
	☐ Exhausted
	☐ Angry
I nourished my body today by eating:	☐ Stressed
	☐ Peaceful
	☐ Happy
I dedicated: _____ minutes/hours to physical activity today.	☐ Unhappy

This energized me at work:

I interacted with these people and felt cared for, motivated and inspired:

I am willing to release:

I showed gratitude by:

I loved this today and will commit to doing more of it:

I showed myself love/care and acceptance by:

I learned this about myself today:

Daily Self-Reflections

I woke up today and felt:

I looked in the mirror and felt:

I nourished my body today by eating:

I dedicated: _____ minutes/hours to physical activity today.

I Feel:
- ☐ Excited
- ☐ Anxious
- ☐ Renewed
- ☐ Exhausted
- ☐ Angry
- ☐ Stressed
- ☐ Peaceful
- ☐ Happy
- ☐ Unhappy

This energized me at work:

I interacted with these people and felt cared for, motivated and inspired:

I am willing to release:

I showed gratitude by:

I loved this today and will commit to doing more of it:

I showed myself love/care and acceptance by:

I learned this about myself today:

DATE:

_____

Daily Self-Reflections

	I Feel:
I woke up today and felt:	☐ Excited ☐ Anxious
I looked in the mirror and felt:	☐ Renewed ☐ Exhausted ☐ Angry
I nourished my body today by eating:	☐ Stressed ☐ Peaceful ☐ Happy
I dedicated: _____ minutes/hours to physical activity today.	☐ Unhappy

This energized me at work:

I interacted with these people and felt cared for, motivated and inspired:

I am willing to release:

I showed gratitude by:

I loved this today and will commit to doing more of it:

I showed myself love/care and acceptance by:

I learned this about myself today:

DATE: _____

Daily Self-Reflections

I woke up today and felt:	**I Feel:**
	☐ Excited
	☐ Anxious
I looked in the mirror and felt:	☐ Renewed
	☐ Exhausted
	☐ Angry
I nourished my body today by eating:	☐ Stressed
	☐ Peaceful
	☐ Happy
I dedicated: _____ minutes/hours to physical activity today.	☐ Unhappy

This energized me at work:

I interacted with these people and felt cared for, motivated and inspired:

I am willing to release:

I showed gratitude by:

I loved this today and will commit to doing more of it:

I showed myself love/care and acceptance by:

I learned this about myself today:

DATE:

_____

Daily Self-Reflections

	I Feel:
I woke up today and felt:	☐ Excited
	☐ Anxious
I looked in the mirror and felt:	☐ Renewed
	☐ Exhausted
	☐ Angry
I nourished my body today by eating:	☐ Stressed
	☐ Peaceful
	☐ Happy
I dedicated: _____ minutes/hours to physical activity today.	☐ Unhappy

This energized me at work:

I interacted with these people and felt cared for, motivated and inspired:

I am willing to release:

I showed gratitude by:

I loved this today and will commit to doing more of it:

I showed myself love/care and acceptance by:

I learned this about myself today:

Daily Self-Reflections

I woke up today and felt:	**I Feel:**
	☐ Excited
	☐ Anxious
I looked in the mirror and felt:	☐ Renewed
	☐ Exhausted
	☐ Angry
I nourished my body today by eating:	☐ Stressed
	☐ Peaceful
	☐ Happy
I dedicated: _____ minutes/hours to physical activity today.	☐ Unhappy

This energized me at work:

I interacted with these people and felt cared for, motivated and inspired:

I am willing to release:

I showed gratitude by:

I loved this today and will commit to doing more of it:

I showed myself love/care and acceptance by:

I learned this about myself today:

Daily Self-Reflections

I woke up today and felt:

I Feel:

☐ Excited
☐ Anxious

I looked in the mirror and felt:

☐ Renewed
☐ Exhausted
☐ Angry

I nourished my body today by eating:

☐ Stressed
☐ Peaceful
☐ Happy

I dedicated: _____ minutes/hours to physical activity today.

☐ Unhappy

This energized me at work:

I interacted with these people and felt cared for, motivated and inspired:

I am willing to release:

I showed gratitude by:

I loved this today and will commit to doing more of it:

I showed myself love/care and acceptance by:

I learned this about myself today:

Daily Self-Reflections

I woke up today and felt:

I looked in the mirror and felt:

I nourished my body today by eating:

I dedicated: _____ minutes/hours to physical activity today.

I Feel:
- ☐ Excited
- ☐ Anxious
- ☐ Renewed
- ☐ Exhausted
- ☐ Angry
- ☐ Stressed
- ☐ Peaceful
- ☐ Happy
- ☐ Unhappy

This energized me at work:

I interacted with these people and felt cared for, motivated and inspired:

I am willing to release:

I showed gratitude by:

I loved this today and will commit to doing more of it:

I showed myself love/care and acceptance by:

I learned this about myself today:

DATE:

_____

Daily Self-Reflections

I woke up today and felt:	**I Feel:**
	☐ Excited
	☐ Anxious
I looked in the mirror and felt:	☐ Renewed
	☐ Exhausted
	☐ Angry
I nourished my body today by eating:	☐ Stressed
	☐ Peaceful
	☐ Happy
I dedicated: _____ minutes/hours to physical activity today.	☐ Unhappy

This energized me at work:

I interacted with these people and felt cared for, motivated and inspired:

I am willing to release:

I showed gratitude by:

I loved this today and will commit to doing more of it:

I showed myself love/care and acceptance by:

I learned this about myself today:

DATE: _____

Daily Self-Reflections

I woke up today and felt:

I looked in the mirror and felt:

I nourished my body today by eating:

I dedicated: _____ minutes/hours to physical activity today.

I Feel:

☐ Excited
☐ Anxious
☐ Renewed
☐ Exhausted
☐ Angry
☐ Stressed
☐ Peaceful
☐ Happy
☐ Unhappy

This energized me at work:

I interacted with these people and felt cared for, motivated and inspired:

I am willing to release:

I showed gratitude by:

I loved this today and will commit to doing more of it:

I showed myself love/care and acceptance by:

I learned this about myself today:

DATE:

_____

Daily Self-Reflections

I woke up today and felt:	**I Feel:**
	☐ Excited
	☐ Anxious
I looked in the mirror and felt:	☐ Renewed
	☐ Exhausted
	☐ Angry
I nourished my body today by eating:	☐ Stressed
	☐ Peaceful
	☐ Happy
I dedicated: _____ minutes/hours to physical activity today.	☐ Unhappy

This energized me at work:

I interacted with these people and felt cared for, motivated and inspired:

I am willing to release:

I showed gratitude by:

I loved this today and will commit to doing more of it:

I showed myself love/care and acceptance by:

I learned this about myself today:

DATE:

_____

Daily Self-Reflections

I woke up today and felt:

I looked in the mirror and felt:

I nourished my body today by eating:

I dedicated: _____ minutes/hours to physical activity today.

I Feel:

☐ Excited
☐ Anxious
☐ Renewed
☐ Exhausted
☐ Angry
☐ Stressed
☐ Peaceful
☐ Happy
☐ Unhappy

This energized me at work:

I interacted with these people and felt cared for, motivated and inspired:

I am willing to release:

I showed gratitude by:

I loved this today and will commit to doing more of it:

I showed myself love/care and acceptance by:

I learned this about myself today:

Daily Self-Reflections

I woke up today and felt:	**I Feel:**
	☐ Excited
	☐ Anxious
I looked in the mirror and felt:	☐ Renewed
	☐ Exhausted
	☐ Angry
I nourished my body today by eating:	☐ Stressed
	☐ Peaceful
	☐ Happy
I dedicated: minutes/hours to physical activity today.	☐ Unhappy

This energized me at work:

I interacted with these people and felt cared for, motivated and inspired:

I am willing to release:

I showed gratitude by:

I loved this today and will commit to doing more of it:

I showed myself love/care and acceptance by:

I learned this about myself today:

Daily Self-Reflections

I woke up today and felt:	**I Feel:**
	☐ Excited
	☐ Anxious
I looked in the mirror and felt:	☐ Renewed
	☐ Exhausted
	☐ Angry
I nourished my body today by eating:	☐ Stressed
	☐ Peaceful
	☐ Happy
I dedicated: _____ minutes/hours to physical activity today.	☐ Unhappy

This energized me at work:

I interacted with these people and felt cared for, motivated and inspired:

I am willing to release:

I showed gratitude by:

I loved this today and will commit to doing more of it:

I showed myself love/care and acceptance by:

I learned this about myself today:

DATE:

_____

Daily Self-Reflections

I woke up today and felt:	**I Feel:** ☐ Excited ☐ Anxious
I looked in the mirror and felt:	☐ Renewed ☐ Exhausted ☐ Angry
I nourished my body today by eating:	☐ Stressed ☐ Peaceful ☐ Happy
I dedicated: _____ minutes/hours to physical activity today.	☐ Unhappy

This energized me at work:

I interacted with these people and felt cared for, motivated and inspired:

I am willing to release:

I showed gratitude by:

I loved this today and will commit to doing more of it:

I showed myself love/care and acceptance by:

I learned this about myself today:

Daily Self-Reflections

	I Feel:
I woke up today and felt:	☐ Excited
	☐ Anxious
I looked in the mirror and felt:	☐ Renewed
	☐ Exhausted
	☐ Angry
I nourished my body today by eating:	☐ Stressed
	☐ Peaceful
	☐ Happy
I dedicated: ___ minutes/hours to physical activity today.	☐ Unhappy

This energized me at work:

I interacted with these people and felt cared for, motivated and inspired:

I am willing to release:

I showed gratitude by:

I loved this today and will commit to doing more of it:

I showed myself love/care and acceptance by:

I learned this about myself today:

"Self-care is not
self-indulgence,
it is self-preservation."

~Audre Lorde

Thoughts & Feelings

Thoughts & Feelings

_____

_____

_____

_____

_____

_____

_____

_____

_____

_____

_____

_____

_____

_____

_____

_____

_____

_____

_____

_____

_____

Thoughts & Feelings

Thoughts & Feelings

Thoughts & Feelings

Thoughts & Feelings

Thoughts & Feelings

Thoughts & Feelings

Thoughts & Feelings

Thoughts & Feelings

_____

_____

_____

_____

_____

_____

_____

_____

_____

_____

_____

_____

_____

_____

_____

_____

_____

_____

_____

_____

_____